JANUSZ PODLECKI
WIELICZKA
A ROYAL SALT MINE

The salt mines of Wieliczka are no less magnificent than the Egyptian pyramids,
but more useful. They are an illustrious reminder of the industry of the Poles.

Le Laboureur, 1647

THE WIELICZKA SALT MINE – TOURIST ROUTE Ltd.

JANUSZ PODLECKI

WIELICZKA
A ROYAL SALT MINE

Introduction
by STANISŁAW ANIOŁ

PUBLISHING HOUSE „KARPATY" – ANDRZEJ LACZYNSKI
CRACOW 1997

The traditional miners' blessing greets everybody who wishes to visit the subterranean labyrinth of the Wieliczka Salt Mine.

The unique character and beauty of the mine was created by nature about twenty million years ago. The Wieliczka salt deposit was formed after the waters of a Miocene sea had evaporated, and its interesting geological structure is the result of the later uplift of the Carpathian Mountains: it is the block type in the upper stratum and the stratified type in the lower one. The Wieliczka Mine also boasts the largest known specimen of Miocene mineralogy: the Crystal Caves. The natural caverns 80 metres under the earth surface display brilliant halite crystals, their edges sometimes 50 centimetres long. The caves were discovered in the late nineteenth century; they have lost some of the crystals (the largest set of crystals from the Wieliczka caves is to be found in Vienna and weighs almost a ton) but visitors are nevertheless spellbound by their beauty. The caves, which are about three kilometres away from the underground tourist route, are strictly protected, as one of the major attractions of the mine.

Although the tradition of salt-mining in the vicinity of Wieliczka goes back about 5,000 years, that is to the Neolithic period, the archaeological evidence concerning settlement in the area does not suggest that the local population grew rich before the eleventh century. A significant development of Wieliczka took place between the eleventh and the thirteenth century, which is corroborated by the charter granted to the settlement about 1289 by the Duke of Silesia and Cracow, Henry IV Probus. The Franconian law charter was confirmed and extended by Duke Przemysł II in 1290.

Obtaining salt from brine must have been fairly developed as the brine well discovered near the present Daniłowicza Street is dated to the twelfth century. Surface salt springs must have become exhausted, which led to constructing wells and drawing up brine. This way of exploiting salt waters seems to have led to the discovery of rock-salt. The oldest known and located Goryszowski shaft which began to mine rock-salt was built in the second half of the thirteenth century. The continuous struggle of man with the nature of the Wieliczka deposit has been going ever since.

The Wieliczka Mine reflects the achievement of simple miners, of Polish kings and of eminent scientists which has taken seven centuries; it portrays the development of technology and labour, as well as the history of the microsociety which evolved around the oldest mining establishment in Europe.

The Wieliczka Mine was always the property of the ruler who entrusted it to the loyal men or leased it out. The proceeds from salt under the Piast and Jagiellon kings provided almost 1/3 of the royal revenue. In the mid-fourteenth century King Casimir the Great codified the unwritten law of the country, which also meant that the rights of the miners who worked "grey gold" became regulated by statute.

The miners at Wieliczka slowly but steadily came to know the mine and discovered its secrets and abundance. The caverns left by mining salt were given timber supports, and the water which flew into the mine was treated to produce salt. In the seven centuries of mining, 7.5 million cubic metres of salt have been extracted, which is equivalent to a train measuring about 1/5 of the length of the equator.

The Wieliczka Mine has nine working floors: from the first one, at 64 metres underground, to the last one, at the depth of 327 metres. The total length of galleries is almost 250 kilometres.

Stubbornly but humbly, the miners quarried salt, constructed drawing machines, and harnessed horses to transport yielded salt. Blocks of salt were hollowed from inside so that a layer of intact rock-salt was left, which for centuries withstood the pressure of the rock mass. The works on one such block often lasted for several generations of miners.

The skills of the Wieliczka miners were well known in medieval Europe. Still, each descent into the mine was hazardous: work there was very dangerous, many miners were killed, and even more suffered injuries. In the sixteenth century almost 10 per cent of the workforce fell victim to accidents. Already in 1363 the Holy Spirit hospital for miners was opened at Wieliczka.

Their dangerous work made the miners more religious than other social groups. The custom has survived of erecting a cross at the spot where a miner perished. Chapels were constructed underground and services said. When in 1697 a chapel was consumed by fire, a royal commission forbade to furnish chapels with inflammable pictures and statues. Paradoxically, this prohibition resulted in developing the unique tradition of rock-salt sculpture which has been kept up in the mine for three centuries. Rock-salt sculptures were carved by miners. The greatest achievement of the self-taught sculptors is the admirable and graceful chapel of the Blessed Kinga, carved 101 metres underground.

According to the legend, the Blessed Kinga, daughter of King Bela IV of Hungary, was responsible for discovering the salt deposit at Wieliczka. On her marriage to the Polish Duke Bolesław the Chaste, she received a salt mine at Marmaros as her dowry. She cast her engagement ring into the shaft of the mine. When on the way to Cracow Kinga's retinue stopped at Wieliczka, she ordered a well to be dug. Yet instead of water, salt was discovered, and in the first lump of salt extracted Kinga's engagement ring was found. Thus the Blessed Kinga became the patroness of salt miners. What seems more likely, however, she introduced comprehensive exploitation in the mine and the royal monopoly of the mining and trading of salt.

There are a number of chapels on the tourist route in the mine. St. Anthony's Chapel on floor I, carved in rock-salt, is seriously damaged but still beautiful. In 1698 mass used to be said there at the beginning of each workday. The Holy Cross Chapel, which has been moved to floor II from an unsafe place, contains one of the few wooden sculptures in the mine, representing Christ Crucified.

In the feeble flame of the miner's lamp, the mine interior seemed dim and mysterious, and imagination animated and magnified everything. Thus a number of tales and legends about

the mine were created. The tales about "Him", or the Warden, who takes care of the miners' safety, are still widely circulated. The Warden has been assigned a chamber on the tourist route in the mine.

All chambers hollowed by generations of miners in the course of seven centuries amount to 2040 workings. We can apprehend the huge size of the mine when having walked along the tourist route we realise that it contains only 3 per cent of all workings.

The first plans of the Wieliczka Mine were produced by Marcin German in 1638, and they were decorated with engravings by Wilhelm Hondius in 1645. It is a rich source of information on the mine at the time and on miners' work. We can see there 'the devil's ride', that is miners sliding down a rope. It was the privilege of senior miners, while the younger ones walked down the mine by stairs and ladders. There are also pictures of the drawing machines on the surface which were operated by horses. In the seventeenth century there were about 100 horses in the mine; they began working there – also underground – in 1620.

Mining rock-salt was a dangerous job but the miners were further threatened by the elements: fire, water and mine gas. Water leaks – the danger miners have been struggling with – frequently threatened the mine and the town built above it. The most recent flooding of the mine in 1992 resulted in serious damage. At present the mine has been coping with over 250 leaks. Fire was a frightful threat, particularly when open flame was used to lighten the mine; it was very serious as fires in a mine were difficult to quench. One of the largest fires, in 1644, raged in the mine for eight month.

Ventilating the mine and the presence of methane, known there as 'saltpetre', were also a major problem. Bellows and pumps were constructed to ventilate the mine, and 'saltpetre' was burnt out by experienced miners who were called 'penitents'. Now the mine is efficiently ventilated by three ventilating systems.

Finally, it must be mentioned that social groups typical of the capitalist system developed early in the Wieliczka Mine. It employed the people who lived in the Wieliczka area and were organised in fairly numerous mining brotherhoods. Run by leaseholders, the mine functioned more or less efficiently. The brotherhoods defended the miners' interests, yet rebellions in the mine occurred from time to time. The most serious of them took place in 1690; it was suppressed by soldiers and ended in a trial followed by death sentences and flogging. Already at the time the miners had a kind of a strike fund, which proves a high degree of organisation among this group of labour. The social phenomena in the Wieliczka Mine preceded similar ones in Europe by about a hundred years.

In 1978 the Wieliczka Salt Mine was entered by the UNESCO on the first list of the World Cultural and Natural Heritage, and in 1994 it was recognised, by a decree of the President of Poland, as a Polish historical monument.

Welcome to the mine, and enjoy and appreciate this unique human achievement – the testimony of human spiritual power, courage and industriousness, humility and passion.

UNDERGROUND GALLERIES, CHAMBERS AND LAKES

A spray chamber owes its fantastic shape to the miners who quarried salt by washing it out from the deposit

The Pieskowa Skała Chamber is the only one on the tourist route which was worked by the pickaxe. Salt was carried up by the simplest hauling device, the hand-operated cross (left)

For centuries salt was picked by hand, loaded into barrels and carried up to the surface

„Carriers" were the miners who carried salt up on their backs or in troughs

The Sielec Gallery; in the Wieliczka Mine horses were used already in the seventeenth century. They carried salt along galleries or were harnessed to treadmills (hauling devices)

A detail of the Erazm Barącz Chamber →

A lake and timbering emphasise the beauty of the Erazm Barącz Chamber (he was the Mine Director under the Austrian rule)

The Gothic form of the timbering in the Michałowice Chamber is the product of the skilled carpentry of the miners →

The Józef Piłsudski Chamber was hollowed in two adjacent salt blocks connected with a small lake. The timber basket structure which holds up the chamber is appreciated by engineers and admired by visitors

The Weimar Chamber (10,000 cubic metres), with a lake, like many chambers in the mine; its size commands respect for the work of the Wieliczka miners

A mine displays the element of earth. The timbering cracks under the pressure of the rock mass and has to be replaced every ten or so years

Brine used to be extracted by the timber mine drainage systems. Now its medical properties are made use of in the underground sanatorium (at the depth of 211 metres)

The Warsaw Chamber (at the depth of 125 metres) is now used for cultural and sports events; it can accommodate about 1000 persons. In the adjacent Vistula Chamber tourists can rest after their underground walk and buy souvenirs, books and special stamps

The Blessed Kinga's Chapel, at the depth of 101 metres (previous page) is a masterpiece created by the miner sculptors: the brothers Józef and Tomasz Markowski, and Antoni Wyrodek. 'The Flight into Egypt' (above) and 'The Miracle at Cana-in-Galilee' are the reliefs carved by Antoni Wyrodek. The high altar with the sculpture of the Blessed Kinga (right) is the work of Józef Markowski and his assistants

The Blessed Kinga's Chapel; the works carved by Józef Markowski in rock-salt: the side altar of the Holy Heart of Jesus and the Resurrection Chapel (above), and (below) Christ Crucified (the sculpture earned an award at the Paris Exhibition in 1901). St. Barbara (below left), the patroness of miners (transparent Wieliczka rock- salt)

Antoni Wyrodek, as the only miner sculptor, was sent to study art in Cracow. In the Blessed Kinga's Chapel he carved in rock-salt, as a self-taught sculptor, the relief 'Christ Preaching in the Temple' (above), and as a professional sculptor, the relief 'Doubting Thomas' (below)

The Blessed Kinga's Chapel; rock-salt reliefs 'Herod's Sentence' (above) and 'The Massacre of the Innocents' (below), by Tomasz Markowski (the younger of the brothers)

The Blessed Kinga's Chapel; Leonardo da Vinci's fresco 'The Last Supper' was the model for the rock-salt relief carved by Antoni Wyrodek who presented it as his diploma work at the Arts Academy. The Bethlehem crib (below) was carved in rock-salt and wood by Józef Markowski

The Blessed Kinga's Chapel; the rock-salt sculptures carved by the Markowski brothers (above): the pulpit, a symbol of the living Polish nation, and the legendary moment of the discovery of the Wieliczka rock-salt deposit. Rock-salt sculptures by Antoni Wyrodek (below): a detail of 'The Flight into Egypt' and the Blessed Kinga

The Nicholas Copernicus Chamber with the sculpture representing the great Polish astronomer, carved in rock-salt by the artist Władysław Hapek (above)
The Janowice Chamber; rock-salt sculpture 'The Great Legend', by the miner Mieczysław Kluzek; it shows the moment of the discovery of the ring which, according to the legend, travelled with salt from Hungary to Wieliczka

'Penitents', sculptures in rock-salt by the miner Mieczysław Kluzek which represent the miners who burn out methane from salt deposits (above and below left). The Casimir the Great Chamber; a bust of the king who was the first in Europe to issue a mining charter (1368), rock-salt sculpture by the artist Władysław Hapek

St. Anthony's Chapel where services at the beginning of each workday were said already in 1698. The sculptures carved in rock-salt by an unknown miner have been partly damaged in the course of time

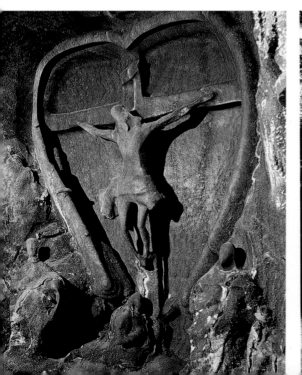

The Holy Cross Chapel, the only timber chapel and sculpture on the tourist route, transferred from an unsafe place in the mine (above). The altar with Christ Crucified in the Margielnik Chamber on floor III (where the new underground tourist route is planned)

For the youngest visitors the miner Stefan Kozik carved in rock-salt a group of gnomes who are believed to help the hard-working Wieliczka miners

'He', the Warden of the Wieliczka Mine, takes care of the safety of the miners and warns them of disasters; rock-salt sculptures by the miners Mieczysław Kluzek and Antoni Cholewa

IN THE LAND
OF SALT CRYSTALS

The Crystal Caves, because of their immense sets of salt crystals, are unique in Miocene mineralogy

The Crystal Caves, located in the block stratum of the Wieliczka Mine (at the depth of about 80 metres), are spectacular because of their beautiful halite crystals, their edges sometimes 50 centimetres long

Water which penetrates the mine is the most dangerous element, but it also adorns the mine as it produces various forms of crystallised salt

Tectonic movements have produced the fascinating patterns of the Wieliczka deposit (above), and salt crystallisation has taken such exquisite forms as 'Kinga's Hair'

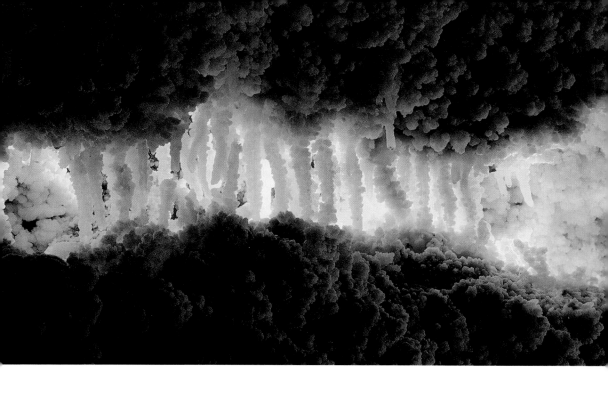

Salt stalactites and stalagmites in the Wieliczka Mine soon merge and produce admirable stalagnates

Photographs and computer processing:
© JANUSZ PODLECKI
in co-operation with:
LETTRA-GRAPHIC Ltd.

Text:
© STANISŁAW ANIOŁ

Editor:
BARBARA ROBAK

Design:
© MAGDALENA MICHALSKA

Translated into English
by JADWIGA PIĄTKOWSKA

First published

ISBN 83-85204-49-0

WYDAWNICTWO „KARPATY" – ANDRZEJ ŁĄCZYŃSKI
30-074 Kraków, ul. Kazimierza Wielkiego 21, tel./fax (0-12) 633-62-13